Peter Maurin
and other poems
by David Craig

Cleveland State University Poetry Center
Cleveland Poets Series No. 40

Acknowledgments

Grateful acknowledgment is made to the following publications, in which poems from this collection first appeared.

Manna: "Iron Fence"
Wellspring: "In Praise of Men (for Marie)"

Thanks to all the people at Madonna House for giving me an example I could never live up to.

The raw material for "Peter Maurin" was gathered from *A Harsh and Dreadful Love* by William Miller, and *Peter Maurin: Gay Believer* by Arthur Sheehan. The woman "Dorothy" mentioned in the poem is Dorothy Day, co-founder of *The Catholic Worker.*

Photograph of Peter Maurin on the cover courtesy of Marquette University Archives.

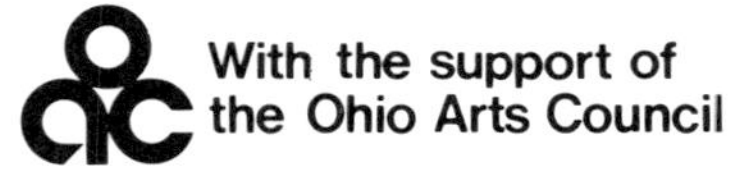

ISBN 0-914946-54-4

Contents

I: Peter Maurin

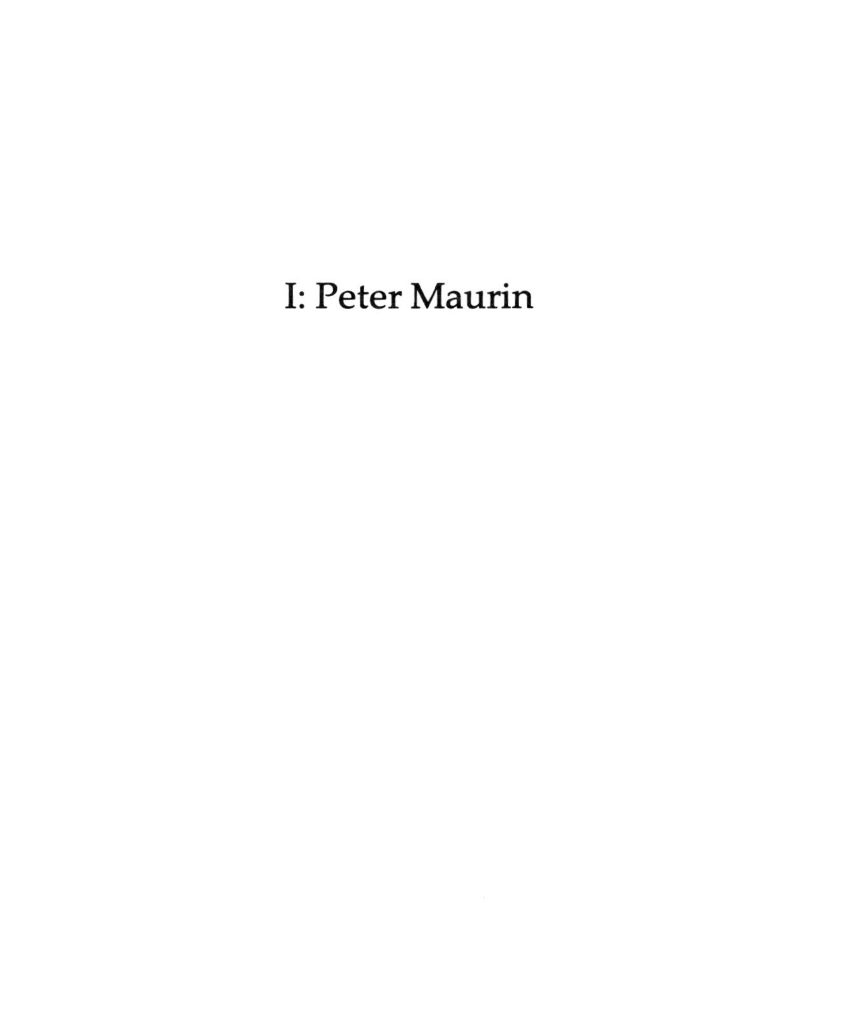

Peter Maurin
(1877-1949)

..if a thing is dull
it is not Christian.
— St. Philip Neri

You are the salt of the earth;
but if salt has lost its taste,
how shall its saltness be
restored?
— Jesus (Mt. 5:13)

First of many children,
twenty one brothers and sisters
in a line   descend on the bean patch
in quadrants sweeping the field
as if on patrol or
scatter   in the early evening,
three on a cow   four in a tree.

Peter ambles toward the statue,
Our Lady   in dark tangles of bush
and then love again   rises like hills after hills
under his ribs   in his eyes,
like a summer morning   white lilies,
dew   incense in the cotton-shaking
of the flowers   rising toward the burning
white-handled sun.

(And that dream:
a familiar robed peasant on his knees groaning,
raising a metal lid over his head
again and again,
digging up the dirt for no apparent reason,
digging.)

The dinner bell and the dark expanse
slowly reclaims the French countryside.   A moon-eye
bright as a child's poppy face
watches   as if the earth were too rare a jewel
to be left unattended.
God's rich brown heart
opening   pierce of apples,
night juice of cooled purple grapes,
the green rinsed valley.

The last one to arrive at the regimented table
he catches the close of the chorus   grace,
the usual games beneath the table   rolling eyes,
all nipped in the span of his father's
regal glance.

At the end of the day when night settles
down   from under the eaves,
he unlatches his bedroom window,
feels its draw.

Peter pumped Dorothy's hand,
had a tie on.

An old coffee stain stretched,
wrinkles smoothed with the working valves.
His shoulders opened like a vault.
"CLARIFICATION OF THOUGHT" echoed through the station
like the slamming of lockers.
A dark patch where money had been,
wrinkles showed that coat's curled value.
"PERSONALIST ACTION" thumped down stairs
entangled strangers.
His broad head contained pines   junkyards,

his eyes tread silver waters   carried
the weight of men
hanged   black stones from the red sleeves of an oak.
Grey hair   a horde of night birds
in the grating of a gathering tree.
Leather worker's skin   sun-gouged,
forded rivers   steel bands
around the mountains.
"VOLUNTARY POVERTY....AGRONOMIC UNIVERSITIES....
THE PROPER USE OF PROPERTY."   Worn left heel,
pantleg pinned.   "PACIFISM."
Shoes   companion to the soil.

Maurin didn't mention the night before,
thoroughly socialized kids
not letting him sleep.
Their powdered mother   mildly annoyed,
"Leave the poor man alone."
"Why don't those people work anyway."

(The wind outside
worked the columns like a plunger.)

Poke of night stick.
"What train, may I ask, are you waiting for?"
I.D. checks   he'd take a lecture   offer
CLARIFICATION.

There were the stories:
1)
Plastic ripped through staples
as wind searched the building   a hand
rummaging through a slatted crate,
    careened down the street   into
        the night   cold stars   the Mother's call

in tall grass.
Maurin stood in that field,
raised his arms   an opening hand
fit that glove
with vatic   flaming fingers.

He had it   that
chested pearl.

Her eyes   watery
asked about “a good time.”
(They shone at being wanted,
not at being taken.
Then they held vats
stirred by an exquisitely
bored hand.   She would feel
contempt   in two.
Men   caves   mouths,
reduced to their needs.

“It’s only a body,” snow
covering the room.)

Peter asked her in   offered
a green and foam chair,
clarified what “a good time”
meant to him,

“...and can I say I know what a good time is
if I don’t live that which I say I know?....”

2)
Jesuit   John LaFarge   1937,
walking down the rat-gnawed cut of a Harlem street toward
a storefront hospitality center,

congregation of brethren down the
bottom of fire escapes.
The coax of bones,
(great brown apple
curving in the icy void)
five on the hoo-hand.   The extended
harangue in a winner's laugh.

Revival.
Storefront Pentecostal church:
door open   door of light.

"Ezekiel saw dem dry bones..."
The sweet slide in virgin voices   falling out,
dancing on the hot planks of pure emotion.
Hands clapping faster   the mingle of praises.

Neighborhood sounds:
a yell a couple of streets over   boys
lean and draped on stoop railing,
a woman's voice
and slamming door up and
down some hallway.

LaFarge looked up at the night sky
saw no Old Testament storm.
    Perhaps it was already here.
    Harlem   sharp glint in the brown opening
    of the eye.
He saw no clouds glowing with fire   coals.
No angels with four faces:
man   lion   ox   eagle.
    The only lions   the buildings,
    toothless   gnawing the air   couched in the dark
    on stringy cords of haunch beneath

razor white stars.
There were no cloven feet.
No eyes on the rims of great wheels.
The only wheels here collided with potholes,
rattled a sorry carriage   a can of screws.

He wondered   "What scrolls had Peter eaten?
what honey tasted?"

There was a valley,
but if an army was going to rise up it would
not come from dismembered bones.
It would be the aboriginal,
aristocratic   bronze-wristed fist....

His heart sank.
There was no electricity   no money
for candles.
But then   in the streetlight,
he could make out a finger   Peter's
and a faint sound like voices.
The stirring of reeds
along a Babylonian canal.

3)
"So he goes to Notre Dame, the guest of
this big philosopher, Emmanuel Chapman
ya see, and the meeting, the meeting
goes fine.   Smooth as a baby's butt.   So
anyway, later, at the bus station Peter
gets to talking and forgets which bus
he's boarding.   Instead of getting on the
bus for Cincinnati he gets on the one
going to Cleveland.   Talk about a death
wish.   Anyway, someone points it out to

him. And he says, are you ready for
this? So he says, he says, 'That's al-
right....I know people in Cleveland!'"
(sound of chair falling over)

Night time:
communal pot twining breath,
four-fingered gloves and overhead white nails.
A chinook blasted the icy slope,
shook the lamentable tract the road,
with the flapping of drum skins.

The chatter of expectant workers tin plates.
They dug in at the foot of ancient stone sheaves,
mountains a turning universe.

Peter took the moment
wrapped it in a blanket:
streets garbage trucks hanging laundry,
in the form of back to back,
sleeping drunks.
It was man's place that occupied him.
He walked with God in leaf-white breeze:
the five-fingered spread white apple bite,
the place of pure projection.
He sailed mystic waters from the walls and windows,
blossoms floating on water through his
fired veins.

"Let the fire spread
hand to steel to
hand."

There was work in Alberta wheatfields   the ditch
and shovel of the Canadian Pacific.
Stone to be quarried   Pharoah's work   in Ottawa.
Concrete forms   like affectations
to be torn down,
and in Akron   buildings   a Godly life
to be constructed.
There were lead mines in Iowa.   Work
as a freight handler   stone and tong with other men
on a boat between Chicago and Muskegan, Michigan.
In Detroit he worked   cold mornings in the yards
of the Michigan Railroad.
Muddy lumberyards.   A sawmill.
Syrup factory.
In a Chicago apartment house   dry
goods store   and   for five years
without pay   maintenance
in an upstate New York summer camp.

Direction.
Peter found his friend   dead
in the Canadian snow:
body twisted   feet tangled in wire and grass,
rifle's accidental discharge and
dark starburst
in the homesteader's chest.

He locked their cabin   left.
Ash on the snow and   inside
he felt the vein-deep,
gleaming till   the plow and wave.

In 1912 found work in Pa. coal country,
lived in unused coke oven
(adjacent oven in operation).

It was warm and dry and his roommate
did the cooking.

He settled in Chicago as a janitor   1925
when the furrow was filled.
Great iron rungs heeded his climbing
air turned in soft billows and the golden
loam on the water spoke
in voices of gulls circling rock and
burnished shore.

You could find him most days at the *Worker*
rooming with the other guests   one-armed   taped
glasses hanging from his nose.

New York.
Under Depression
years   he worked without pay
at the half-filled summer camp.
Given a weekend dollar Peter was off:
NYC library to read   Union Square
to wrangle with the radicals.
At night   he'd get a bed at Uncle Sam's
on the Bowery,
give up the bed   take
to good wood   vertebrae falling
in skeletal descent   a line against the floor
like a progression of summer shoes
down summer steps.

The essays.
Easy Essays   written over the ruts,
Bowery coffeehouse tables   lanternlight,
hay and barn near Kingston NY   on benches
above gathering pigeons   next to sleeping drunks,
Union Square.

Dorothy saw him once
in a gap-toothed picket line,
German consul's office   take out a faded green
notebook   lick the lead and
isolate
while his sign   protesting Nazi "Achtung Juden"
drooped as he walked absently
along in line.

At home.
Peter   morning in rags   yellow beamed,
laughed   carried the "business manager" away.
(Icicles melting from the corner of a cottage roof,
spears knee deep in the snow.   The large crack in river ice.)
He'd get a buck and swing the door open
wide: noonday Mass in high arching corridor,
echo of kneeler,
St. Francis of Assisi church;
bop to the Bowery   breakfast stew for a pair of cool
dimes.   Then he'd go walking slowly,
teacher   bullet-eyed   hands behind his back,
Union Square   pockets packed with pamphlets.

He agreed with a concentration
camp priest who once said that
man's freedom was so precious
that no one should ever exert
a personal influence to win
another to an idea, that it was
the truth alone that should
attract.

Eyes on you   Peter said what you had to hear.
Listening was your baggage.
He gave love without sympathy because sympathy

was not love.
He learned   simply
to always go to God.
He never passed a hungry man   gave away coats,
socks   said workers should wash the guest's feet,
the guest having already offered a freeing hand.

The burning.
"I have written enough.   It is time for
the young people to take over."

And for five years
leaves fell off the tree.

He was taken to Mott Street for winter but
when the red-throated white-rimmed blossoms appeared
Peter was brought to the farm   rocking
chair in the yard.
Slowly   crab apples came to bud   the gentle
rain of snow white calendar leaves
spiraled toward the grass.
He smiled,
out with the birds.
Hills   like angry bears rose
in the distance.

In the summer of '48 he sat quietly beneath the pines,
attended.

The previous April he had disappeared.
Workers reached every corner of the district:
dives   subways,
called distant friends.
He appeared   four days later without words.
They put a note in his pocket,

"I am Peter Maurin, founder of the Catholic Worker Movement."

Coda.
He sat by the fire
oblivious to the priest's remark,
"Peter's love is the stove."
Caught in the burning,
a holocaust.
(Perhaps for some American family,
that they might learn to give
not out of their excess,
but into their need,
that their hearts   sides   might remain open,
unhealed   for the Son
room.)

Dorothy   before going to a funeral
told him,   "You'll have a friend in heaven."
Peter's smile replaced the pain,
the endurance that had etched his face.
On the way back   she got the call from Mary Farm,
dark starburst.

She went to the Chapel   walked
slowly toward the Virgin.
Tears   a thousand flickering tongues   burning
for the wealthy   for the wielders of clubs   for a
New Jerusalem.

He was laid out in a donated suit,
brothers and sisters
in a line.

Dorothy recalled with some irritation
how visitors had spoken to him as if he were a toddler.
This poor man's mind   last possession,
gone.

II. Apple Fools

The Peeling

Mostly there is the wait
you stand there as if at a tailor's   God
peels you like an onion
thin pages   a clouded glass

Women   hundreds of eyes
brown and rich as a surge of soil
bright as a pillow   the moonlight
Every game passes   ego
peeled away like your pink skin

And still   there you stand because
what could you give for this?
Your eyes in an outstretched hand?
A hollow skull tone?

I Saw All the Forgiven

I saw all the forgiven
in a wide opened cathedral
I saw banners waving
shouting   praising

I saw the forest darken
as we   zipped and sweaty   dirt biked
roared flaps up   through water
tailed in sand

I saw the bottle-necked sun
tincture red   set
I saw clouds turn red as I sat barefooted
on a shingled roof

Iron Fence

twenty furred young sparrows tuck
on a cold young tree
next to the old black stone church downtown
buildings and a crunchy blue sky

people scurry   it's six degrees
a stoplight waits beyond
this cold pointed black iron fence

Halfway Up

Praise and narrow
is the way

My Own rejoices in a Kansas barn
in the dust   sledge   shredding planks
in the spreading sunlight

With His eyes   halfway up
I see the gold   the trees   the sky
that old beat pick-up
coming small
up the road

The Presence of God

He spoke in a thimble
a choir of pigeons   necking about
long peals   rakes of ice   railroad tracks
in front of toothless builings   hollow
corridor smiles and the
bite in frozen grass

up they flew
and over
me and every spider wire

a cold hissing   soft
under the flap
and feather of muscled wings

Pentecost:

Who is this Holy Spirit?
And what is He doing in the eggplant?

Your Feet

(for Susan)

I never knew I
carried your smile

would want to bury myself
in black wet soil

could kiss God's soft mouth
that He would kiss me back

but I always knew
I'd want to wash your wide feet

Reflection: 105 Degrees

Yes
these rough fingers would hold the flow
of your kinked at the roots   island hair

I would watch you   crooked woman
like water fountaining from the hose
carry you on sun wheels up driveways
with buckets of gravel
like I do my stalk green self   shovel shine in
a fan of water from the shearing
the friction in a half ton of that stone

Come   there are basements to rip out
chunks of concrete and the singe of hot metal
forearms from the inside of dump truck doors
There are trenches to be dug
Plastic pipe and sump pumps to be sunk
There is beer after

Tonight I look up   through the skylight
from the kitchen table   say
"I will sweep the corners of this great night
bone   wipe the little windows clean."

First Poem

Linda   movies
pearl nights with a grain of freight high
in the dark roll of the clouds
and a pier ending
in the talk of water

leaves and streetlight
I can give you that

I can give you maple skies   shots of yellow leaf
matched   in the limes of where you've been
to stallions snorting in the frost on wider
horizons   in the pinwheel glaze of autumn
the marshalled wren who walks on brown leaves
swims this ancient breeze

I can give you that

Apple Fools

Apple fools   we are
Ripe as cups of cider and the horse's
clodded wake

let the wet mornings come   ring out
green beans beneath the leaves   pumpkin
piping on the vine
Speckled corn aloft   Indian feathered
high on the door

Squash squats on the rafters
pot belly   bent legged   Buddha stove
boots and coveralls
Give us this grace and all this day
the crowded table the
pinions' fold

Ash Wednesday

(Puerto Rico)

the treed hills   carpet green
cows slipped in and out of view

Under plywood roof
mismatched chairs   table and a breeze
coconut's milk   pianono
You canvassed my past   I watched you move
Children   three on a bike   sounded the asphalt
through palms and flourish of undergrowth

the ocean was green...

you were beautiful

we met in moccasin   season
our completion smoothed us like stone

At night the ocean rolled
without distraction
(we could have been the shore)
Sand like glass
stars and an arching moon

You wanted to make love on the beach
I said   you to me   forever

Assumption:

outside this chalked church window
fields foam yellow
water rattles like children over
gaunt grey shoes   stones
Clouds   frigates
steam past

inside   Ian holds the paten
his eyes are blue
and   at ten   they run like cold northern waters
He follows each creak as if he had talons

I go up with John   Barb
holds the chalice
A whole line goes up   all the workers
and Stroh burners
the blue-bellied captain of the bazaar tent team
goes up
minus the swagger and the boom
goes up with his wife and retarded daughter
who is big and childlike   clean   shaven

Genesis: chapter one

When the morning is spread out before you
and it's your first morning

When the fat apples bend the boughs
your first breeze rustles the first leaves
and shafts of sunlight catch the curve of birds

Then your heart   your heart
leaps with river water
over handstand rocks   up and into
bottled blue

Gospel Poem #1

Jesus
Loaded Jowl Cakes   Mother of seismic dreams
if only I could touch Your pebbled face
Coax the clamshell
lunch time read-out
Come   take the owl from the pumpkin   march
the skins of the old days out the necessary door
You are the Mother walker   candle tongue
bee thread   Take the lies
exchange them for jazz on Barnaby street
flower the walls with tutors of lost languages
Let me shout Your blare-root
over the beams of every mule house
Come   Come   Come
in a munch of apples in
every trumpet's blaze through keys of ivy
under sun-dusted sleeves

Gospel Poem #2

Jesus
Good Friday   blood on the teeth   night a
steel trap   Blades of amber grass
The stoney reach of cliffs along Herod's lacquered pate
The blue ranches within Your mortgaged veins
angry house   licensed ache
Your fibula   now cow's head along Nebraskan roads
Call on us   dead one   we will not answer
Call on us and watch our bruised mouths negotiate
ivory steps   The gears of our gospel survive us
Talk to us of holiness   we were not listening
our hands are angry and run like mice
along our beetled bones

Gospel Poem #3

Jesus
Risen
past the amphibial claws
the promontories of self all
governing bodies   Pious instruments will
chase hatted seeds   Holy files
of presbyters will rejoice   alphabetically
and even the coldest thumb-tied road   unwinds
O Dark Embrace Your
wings   blood-dipped   sun-dipped   curl
around the rumpled cloth the rock hard
earth   Jesus
we hear persimmon voices out over the water
We bud under snowcake   in trees
out over heretical streets
We are the thoughtful seals and our chorus
runs in timber down steel beams
fuels the electron span beneath bankers   billboards
Furnished Ash   we wait

III. Tiny Dances

African Shoes

There are small bone-shaped heads which come up
in the frosted grass   winter mornings
They are the size of African shoes
They are   angels

Large hands rattle the fake fronts
of Western-style buildings

There are angels' wings
in the mountains   They make noises
like old machinery

The metal fence post   the strung barbed wire
become illumined   cold grass burns and
the small voice
passes

Spring, to Work

There is stone in negative earth
As I wait for my bus
buildings   like hands
praise

Sap-In-The-Wood   here   in the suburbs
trees billow green smoke across
a pertinent field

Down the paved   country road
wet bark blossoms in shells and
a mandate of rock costs the stream only time
only hours

Cantaloupe flowers ride the pine
masted   in the tuck
of turtle lake

Up the walk in front of the Detention Home
In pink blossoms
white rafts
blossoms wet on the cattled ground

The Light Behind the Imagination

a yellow taxi
yellow leaves

no calls
and from the spacious front Checker seat
the wrap-around glass
a large tree ahead
Leaves   gone at the top   like a
woman's back   her robe
dropping from the shoulder
(or   leaves   a hive of busy
shivering bees)

off to the right
a tanned shirtless roofer unrolls tarpaper
along a low-pitched roof
The sounds of his hammer
catch the glittering nails
"See this," they say.
"This is what lasts."

In Praise of Men

(for Marie)

Woman tree   shaking out spools of hair
green and yellow leaves   see how across the field
dandelions hold the faces of men who would gladly dance
in your dreams   Tiny portraits dangle   next to strings of
thin clear beads   small Vivaldi
phonographs   See how the hands of men
are like slow moving cattle
how their hair is like piled wood or water
dripping from the eaves   See how they work
See how those arms   awkwardly   gently
hold a baby

. . . Cleveland, Dec.

Driving down Green Rd.
across from the warehouse for the mentally retarded
where I used to work the
field spreads out in
tall   wet   weighted orange grass
the occasional   arms and elbows   adolescent tree
In the distance   a core of bristle an
earthen comb
Trees along the horizon
Seepage   and closer
a ticking in the branches
Grey clouds and a rush of grey hands
beating seasonal drums

Had I pulled over   opened
the door of my green '69 Tempest
stray molding flapping against small brackets
and walked out   squishing in the mud
and a cabin built there
no doubt my days would now be slower
surer   no doubt
I would hear more often
my body and this planet pass
like weather-beaten cars

Roommates (what goes around comes around)

1.
Mark extends a one by one from the chair
to the swing-around porch rail.
His macaw disdains the perch, prefers to be
upside down. Two claws, his beak, one claw.
Then he cracks down to porch level landing
on his beak, proceeds
waddling up Mark's arm using it
to hoist himself up the sleeve.

Mark talks about "granola types,"
"low impact people." I wonder,
"What is he?"

Later, his friends come over, all of them talking
Californian, the same private talk.
Sickened, I slip out during a slide show:
Mark's job, diamond hunting in British Guyana,
and walk up the street, private,
in darkness.

2.
Cee tells me about the LeHigh Valley, her
one brother who cracked up his car in the state park,
walked out of it, in a state of shock and
fell down the embankment to his death, bystanders gawking.
I weed in her garden, tell her I saw three blackbirds
land there and then, at the sight of her pinwheel
on a stick, get up and fly away.
Her laughter reaches the roof, ends
with the dust in the latticework.

Elias

Elias slumped under a Juniper tree

Before he passed out
he tried to tear his shirt
"TAKE MY LIFE
Lord, I am no better than my fathers."

When God bent down to moisten his brow
leave him food
He spoke almost to Himself

"I never said you were."

A Conversation with Tolstoy

(upon reading "The Death of Ivan Illych")

snowflakes settle slowly down
every lust deepens   white
edges up the house

the years   having piled
are slowly absorbed   widened
Old friends probably remember

I ask about this life we live in
he says, "Love whom you are given."

Mentally Retarded:
Case #29061 (Memphis Slim)

Glenn's heading for the University of LaSalle
wants to run in the next Olympics
        an "out-of-state track champ"

When he comes back in the evenings
he holds his face close to yours
so you can see the sweat

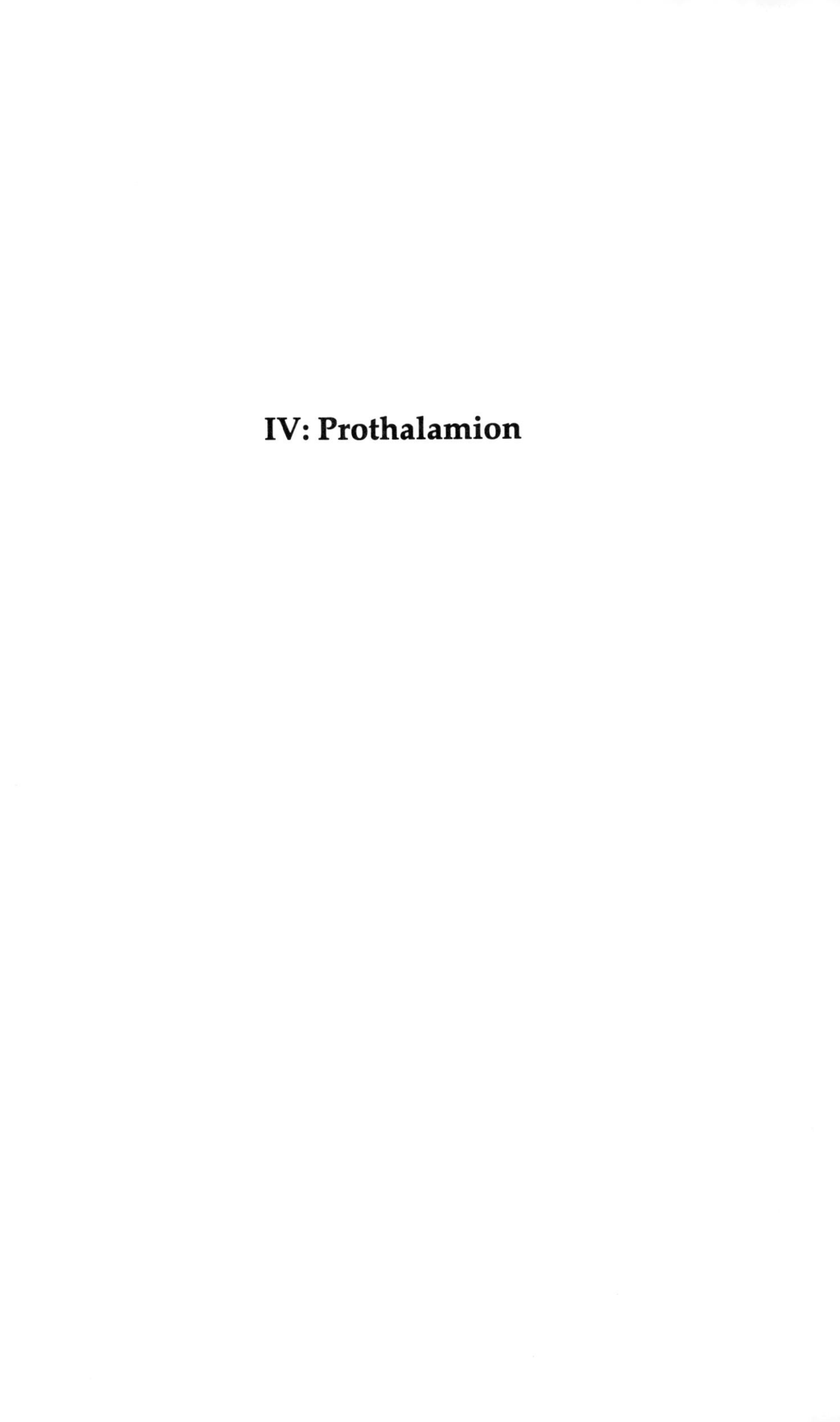

IV: Prothalamion

Prothalamion

"I said shoot the gun Weaver, and Weaver
just laughin' . . ."
— Larry Craig

I.
I remember you brother,
your cheap shag rug $600 delinquent.
"Let 'em come and rip it out,
what are they going to do, wreck my credit?"
Your leaning plywood audio stand,
6 junkers in the yard   none
of them running;   I remember a
drunken brawl   in the kitchen,
you pulling out my hair,
me back to empty my guts   then
a bed of cool grass under water stars,
a hard rock moon.   Yes,
you and all the low riders,
West Side boys   hot banjos,
tool chests;   Casey hitting up all the crank
he could feel into his thumb
like Shirley wouldn't know he was off,
and him circling our dining room   immersed
(by himself) in a three-way conversation.
A motorcycle roared by and
he stopped   looked at me   said,
"Suzuki!,   Yamaha!!,   Kawasaki?!?"
Then he'd grin;   I remember racks of clothes
in back seats of cars: "Step into
my office,"   Jeff   "the original component,"
stealing all that shit from Zayre's
on those overnighters: an empty
cookware box stuffed with jeans,
4 pair for 9 bucks.

Convict Butch and his brother,
that Chinese guy they forced into their truck:
a fetus   for three days;
Danny, you, and Scotty with your
Sportsters: you cracking up with regularity,
your back a sheet of juicy pink;
Scotty   leching because he couldn't
reach out to someone without pulling;
Pay Kinney   proud of his overall
genital length   packing his guitar
for a tow truck   nights
on the interstate;
Craig and Bob Esper: one still
quaking from Army acid trips the
other bound   determined to drink   to sail
his way through the tomb;
Me and Bird   through Quebec down
into Maine past the border guards;
me stuffing her head between my legs
contemptuous of her love   hating her
by the time we got to Boston.

73rd street boys   stacking
case after case of Miller
next to the fridge;   their spun tales
of knocked-off boxcars,
how they busted through the plywood in
your door because it was locked.
(That picture of Jeff standing in the door
half in   half out.)   Your 12 guage
loaded and cocked in the closet;
pistol practice in the living room;
everyone to the stadium for a
Billy Graham crusade   getting saved,
and then   within a week   back at it.

Mike   who wrote to all those leather women;
Red   who talked about how the doctor
drained his arm of hit-up downs,
the fluid filling a small glass;   him
being shot 5 times,
spinning in the bar   slow motion
like an hallucination;
Donna   her 4 abortions   Rhonda,
tripping since she was 9;   and downtown,
Roman from next door   the candy man:
1000 tuinals   pinball wizards off corridor walls;
Danny's baseball friend tossing
a radiator around in the hall;
both Debbies   impromptu gigs on pots and pans,
guitars   Debbie number one   past her bed,
one moon vying with the other:
4 guys   2 women: one in the
bathtub with a soccer player   the other,
on her ass   swishing up to me with her robe
opened to her golden triangle   the sound
ringing in her semiconscious head.

Then Butch killed Jeff   both speeding   shot him
because he wouldn't hand him the phone.

I remember those rooms:
acid: the night streets,
my face pulling in different directions
as if I had comets
inside my skin   shooting   bouncing off
the pink insides   forcing occasional
protrusions of the face   the
teeth grind   feeling metallic;
cords   in my stomach   shook
in waves   like a bridge of bound,

knotted bamboo shoots;   the
general body fuck;   I felt fused
and wanted to take off each of my limbs,
stick them into a garbage can
until they stopped quaking   twisting;
I wanted to get rid of my teeth,
my brain   string my intestines like
dried tripe   from rock ledge
to rock ledge.

How I started talking to Jesus freaks
noticing their eyes;
how I'd rummage those dark streets,
walk over to Pix's in my acid shoes
having cut work   she and the baby and Lee
or go to the house of the wisest man
I knew because Ginsberg had suggested it.

I talked about the walls' temporary nature,
about how they'd all have to come down.
His wife rubbed her arms   left   then,
in a few minutes   he   after her.
I paced his rooms   watched
the dog watch me;
watched it piss on the carpet.   How I left,
how I'd rummage those dark streets waiting
for the chance just
to get out.

II.

"You have not called me.
I have called you."
— Jesus

Walked into the main house dining room
still speeding   the inside of my
elbow discolored   80 people
looking at me and I took a
dinner seat.

Worked on the farm after
morning lauds   after homemade bread
and honey with breakfast.
Someone told me I was eating
too much;   split kindling and through
falling flakes   heard the singing
from the upstairs chapel;
the distant trees looked frosted.
Sorted potatoes with Miles;
assigned to cow's head detail
with Daoud: cut the meat from the
skull   poked its eye with a knife
looking for some ooze;
held sheep with Mike waiting for the
bullet above the forehead, skinned them
punching fists between meat and pelt.
Fed lumbering cows old potatoes,
being bounced around.
The cross planted in stones
at the top of the hill;   sometimes
going up at break;
and once a   horse-drawn sleigh ride.

On off days we'd pillage St. Joseph's
pants for a dime or walk back
through snowy trails   an old deserted
farm deep in the hills,
1947 newspapers in the crumbling rooms;
in the evenings   all the people talking about
Jesus   as if He was their neighbor.
I liked the guy   what he said and who he said
it to but   like   He never rang my doorbell.
They all smiled.

Nights back at the dorm;
fell asleep on my Bible   Mike and Steve
immediately formed Inquisition,
"Boredom with the Word!"

Out and singing carols for the neighbors,
tried to get next to that lady
from Venezuela;   shovelled
the snow into banks off the river
inlet   played with brooms and tennis ball
in boots on the ice   a goal
between barrels on each end;
bounced friends and acquaintances into
the snow;   poetic Byzantine liturgies   high
hats and lots of bowing.
I remember a hermit   how when he met me
he shook my hand   bent it all
the way back   his eyes telling me,
"Be strong."   And before I left that first time,
Father Bob and a nurse   praying over me.
I repeated, "Thank You, Jesus."
until my jaws ached then   finally,
the dove shook my bones with wind and
prophecy   answered every internal

question for 15 minutes or so
completely overriding my analytical mind.

Then, some months later,
went down to Steubenville $45
in my pocket   and a suitcase full of books,
night coming on   knocking on doors;
lived in a monastery   visited Susan
at night   her bare rooms,
small bed   her prophecying   Jesus telling
us to stop;   I remember the tapes she returned,
me whipping them up the street in the dark,
hitting parked cars.

God leading me away to
Redwood Valley   California;
abbey sitting: watched the pigs   peacocks,
chickens   sheep;   Hugh   my compatriot,
a disbarred lawyer   writing bad fiction;
Rose   ex-Hell's Angel junkie prostitute
took me to Indian reservation revivals.
Teeth being filled with gold or
silver or pearl   the blind
sight;   that escaped killer
Soledad refugee   stayed
for awhile: cops at 2 am
banging   too late   on the chapel door,
me   opening it   sleepy-eyed,
looked at 5 pump shotguns;
days weeping after Susan,
seeing her broken in my dreams;
nights and mornings cradled in God's
bright   leafy arms.

Then back to Steubenville   and Liza,
woman to my man;   the union that lived
under my bones;   my proposing 3 times,
her accepting 3 times;   her   a reformed
lesbian   dumped all her man-hate and me
driving her into the Army with my furious wound,
my self-contempt.

All of it turning above
the peace that passeth all understanding
which flowers under sunlight
in my storekeeper's chest.

III.

"No, not I, but Christ
who liveth in me."
— St. Paul

Brother   we are like weeds growing
in the fields.   Our arms,
lettuce for the bees.
As a child   I used to watch you
ride your bike   standing on the seat,
into a fallen telephone pole.
We have grown through the friends
and powers that have peopled our days.
And now   Ragtime   another turning.
May it bring you peace   and children,
realization that we are not here for
ourselves   but for the laying down:
hands to wood   feet to wood.
And may the years that brought you
keep you   and the love that yearns
coal the fires of your handlebar dreams.